DISNEP
MOANA

pi kids®
Phoenix International Publications, Inc.
Chicago • London • New York • Hamburg • Mexico City • Paris • Sydney

Moana is the daughter of the village chief of Motunui. Even as a toddler, she loved hearing Gramma Tala tell how the mother island Te Fiti emerged from the sea long ago. Then, a trickster demigod named Maui stole a sacred stone, the heart of Te Fiti, and awakened the demon Te Kā. The legend says someone must sail beyond the reef, find Maui, and take him to restore the heart of Te Fiti before a darkness takes over Motunui.

Some of Moana's friends find Gramma Tala's story a little too scary. Search the room for these terrified tots:

Moana is drawn to the ocean. Her father Tui warns, "You don't go out there. It's dangerous." But the ocean seems to speak to her. While young Moana plays with the waves, she spies something shining in the water—the heart of Te Fiti! Gramma Tala rescues the stone and keeps it in her shell necklace for safekeeping.

Moana waves to the sea, and it waves back! See if you can spot Moana and these Motunui villagers:

Moana

Tui

Heihei

Gramma Tala

this villager

Pua

Years later, after Gramma Tala gives her the heart of Te Fiti, Moana knows it's her destiny to find Maui and accompany him to return the sacred stone. She takes an ancient canoe—and, accidentally, a rooster named Heihei—and hits the high seas in search of the legendary demigod. When she finds him, he is not at all what she expected. He is not only full of himself, he's full of tattoos that move!

Maui's tattoos tell how he defeated monsters and gave mortals everything from fire to coconuts. Scan the scene for these items from Maui's amazing tales:

Mini-Maui

this coconut

this necklace tooth

eel monster

earthquake god

fire

As Moana and Maui argue about whether or not he'll help her, Moana's boat is attacked by the Kakamora, mean little coconut-armored bandits. To make matters worse, Heihei swallows the heart of Te Fiti, then gets snatched by a Kakamoran warrior. While Maui defends the boat, Moana has to act fast to get the rooster and the stone back!

The Kakamora are surprisingly cute, considering they wield giant, razor-sharp spears! Can you spot these coconutty crooks?

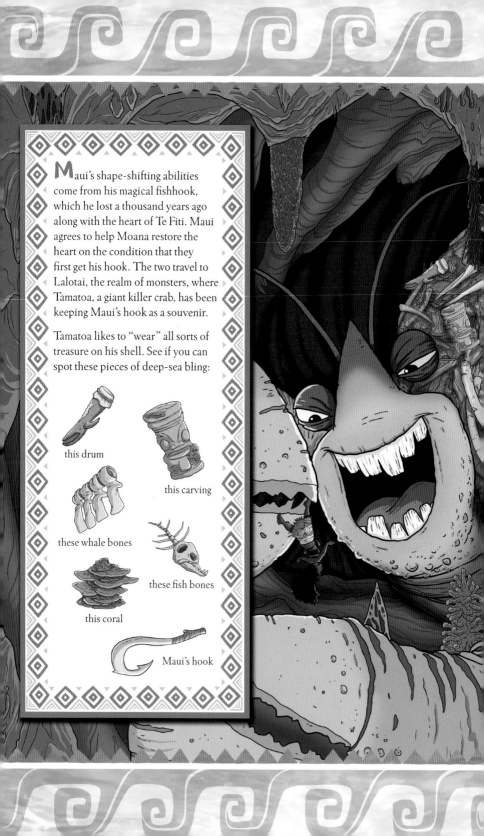

Maui's shape-shifting abilities come from his magical fishhook, which he lost a thousand years ago along with the heart of Te Fiti. Maui agrees to help Moana restore the heart on the condition that they first get his hook. The two travel to Lalotai, the realm of monsters, where Tamatoa, a giant killer crab, has been keeping Maui's hook as a souvenir.

Tamatoa likes to "wear" all sorts of treasure on his shell. See if you can spot these pieces of deep-sea bling:

this drum

this carving

these whale bones

these fish bones

this coral

Maui's hook

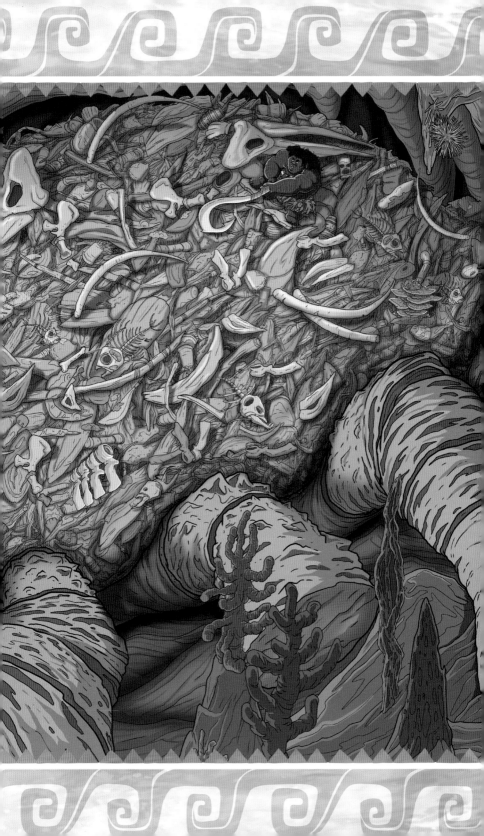

Moana convinces Maui to take on the demon Te Kā and restore the heart of Te Fiti. She sails toward Te Kā even after Maui tells her to turn back, and his hook is cracked in the fierce battle! Angry, Maui leaves with his broken hook. Moana decides to return the heart of Te Fiti herself. The monster hurls lava and boulders as she approaches, but Moana doesn't give up. Fortunately, Maui doesn't give up on her either!

Maui can turn from a bug to a shark to a bird in a flash. Spot him as he shape-shifts from one animal form into another before becoming a hawk and flying over to help his friend:

lizard

pig

shark

beetle

fish

hawk

Moana sails through fiery bursts of lava while Maui confronts Te Kā. Singing the song of her ancestors, Moana gets close enough to return the heart of Te Fiti. Suddenly, the mother island starts to reveal herself! Amid the blooming flowers, Te Fiti returns Maui's hook, which was destroyed in the battle.

As the island paradise begins to bloom, search the lush, green scene for Moana and these creatures and objects:

this sea turtle

glowing heart of Te Fiti

this oar

this crab

Moana

this bird

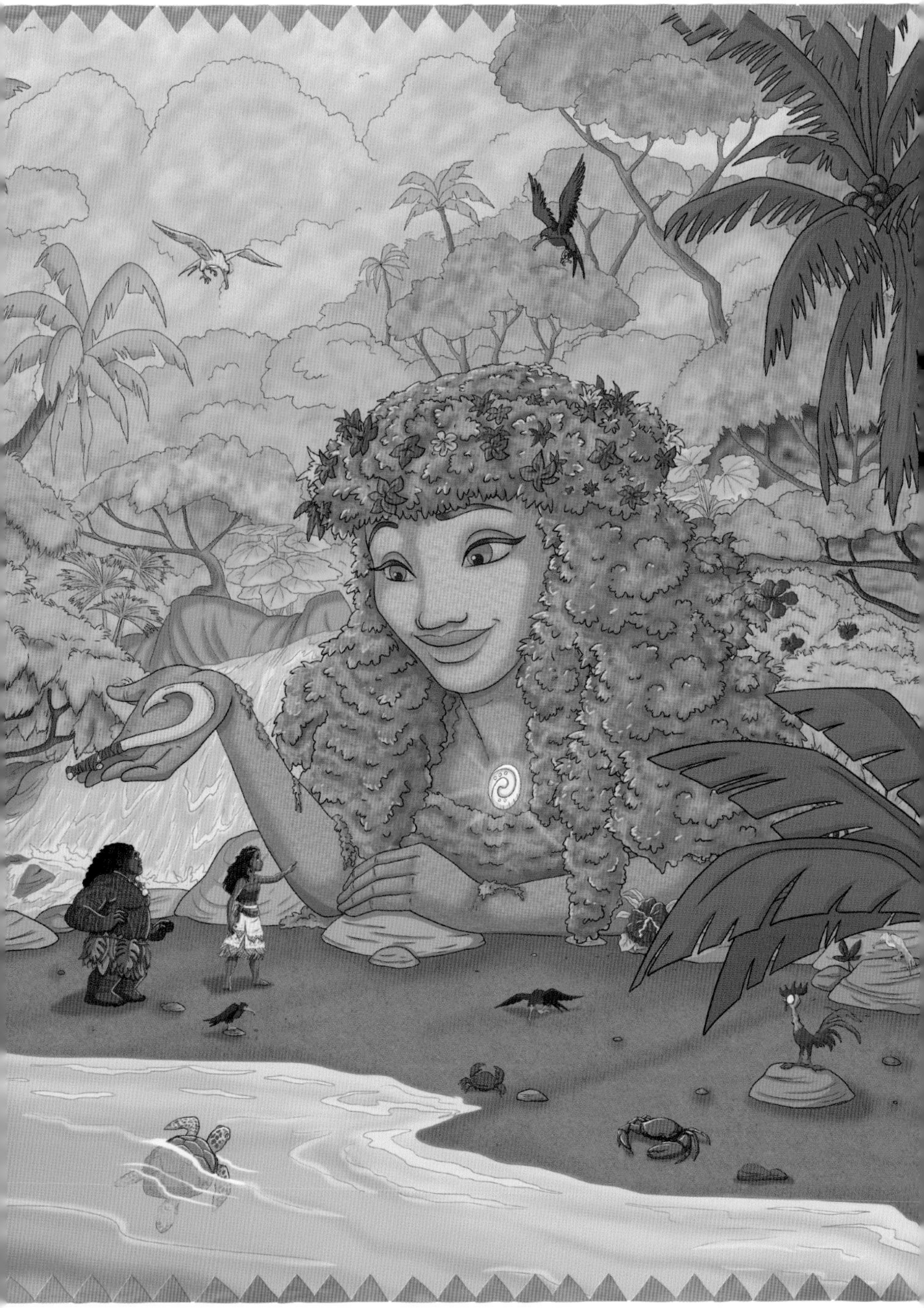

Back in her village, Moana is a hero! She has brought life back to the island and the art of navigation back to her people. Now, she is a master wayfinder, leading other explorers to new lands. The spirit of her ancestors and the love of her friends and family have taught her to always listen to that voice inside her that says, "I am Moana!"

Can you find Moana and these friends and followers as she sets off for new adventures?

Pua

Tui

this sailor

Heihei

Moana

Maui

Toddle back to story time and scan the screens for these mythical monsters:

Roll back to the beach and collect these shells:

Trek back to Maui's tattoos and find these forces and features of nature:

sun

coconut tree

grass

sea

flame

wind

Sail back to the Kakamora scene and locate these weapons:

Dive back down to Lalotai and find this otherworldly undersea architecture:

As Moana sails toward Te Fiti, look for these flying lava bombs and boulders:

Travel back to Te Fiti and search the landscape for this greenery:

Navigate back to Moana's fleet and search for these nautical necessities:

this oar

pennant

anchor

this sail   rope   this oar